I
Turn to
the Light

Also by Connie Bowen

I Believe in Me

I
Turn to
the Light

A Book of Healing Affirmations

Written and Illustrated
by Connie Bowen

UNITY® Books

Unity Village, Missouri

I wish to thank God, the Breath of Life; my husband Mike, who is my rock, my wings, my anchor, and my sun; my child Matthew, the light and joy for which I prayed; all my family and friends, who strengthen and encourage me; and the Unity staff, who through their patience, skill, and dedication shine the light of God ever brighter for us all.—CB

First Edition 1998
A **WeeWisdom**® Book for the Child Within Us All

To receive a catalog of all Unity publications (books, cassettes, compact discs, and magazines) or to place an order, call
the Customer Service Department:
(816) 969-2069 or 1-800-669-0282.

The illustrations in this book were done in black ink and colored pencil.

LIBRARY OF CONGRESS CATALOGING-IN-PUBLICATION DATA

Bowen, Connie.
    I turn to the light / by Connie Bowen. — 1st ed.
      p. cm. — (WeeWisdom book)
    Summary: A series of brief statements designed to help readers feel connected to God.
    ISBN 0-87159-216-9
    1. Spiritual life—Juvenile literature.   2. Unity School of Christianity—Doctrines—
Juvenile literature. [1. Spirituality.]
    I. Title.   II. Series.
    BX9890.U505B69   1998
    248.8′2—dc21

                                      97-32788
                                      CIP
                                      AC

ISBN 0-87159-216-9
Canada BN 13252 9033 RT

For all those who ask for Truth, look no further than oneself.

Introduction

An awareness of the presence of God is the greatest gift we can receive, for God is the creator of all things magnificent. We are the precious children God holds most dear.

By our choosing to quiet the chatter of untruth, both inner and outer, listening to the guidance from within, and following the path of what we find most spiritually nurturing, we open a channel blocked only by our limited thinking.

Read aloud these affirmations and dwell on those that are most comforting. As we align our thinking with Truth, the energy of Love is brought to our awareness and miracles spring forth to bless us.

We can experience our divine nature, live our highest Light, and reflect our inner knowing.

Good fortune awaits you with every breath if you will but turn to the Light of Love.

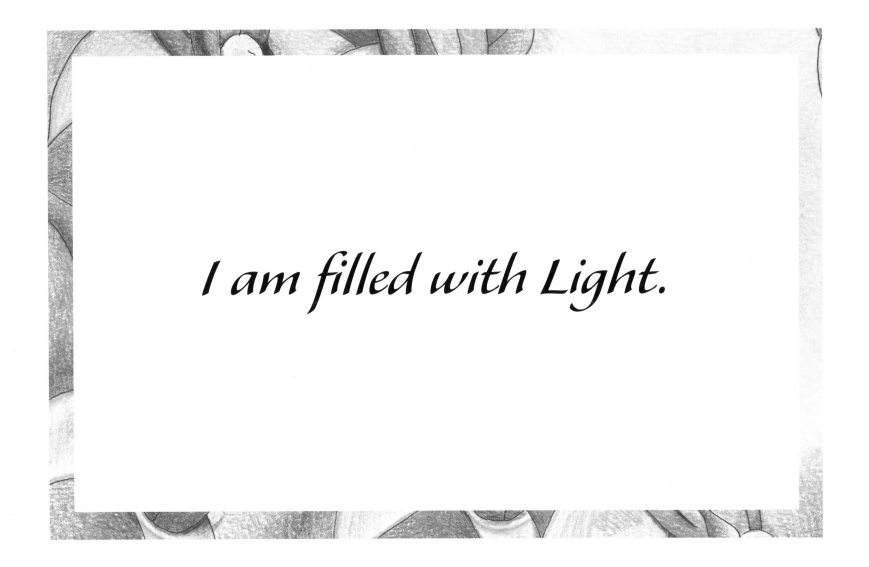

I am filled with Light.

I am one with God.

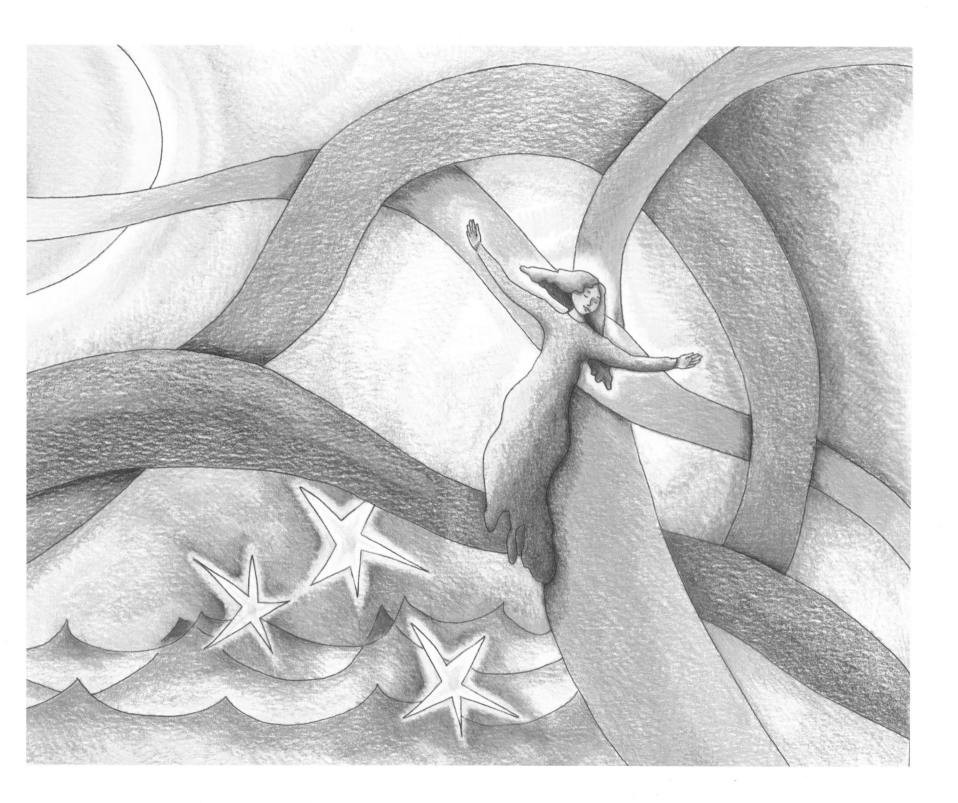

I am made in the image of
the Most High.

I feel the divine spark of Light, comfort, and warmth within me.

Faith is the door through which God speaks to me.

In my heart,
I know what is right for me.

All my choices reflect the Light.

*I allow myself
to follow my dream.*

I choose the path paved in miracles.

Fear holds an empty promise.

I choose Love.

My heart is open to Love.

God's love
flows through me now.

God's love in me knows

the Truth.

I am the glorious gift of God.

I release all limiting beliefs;
there is but one Power.

I am free.

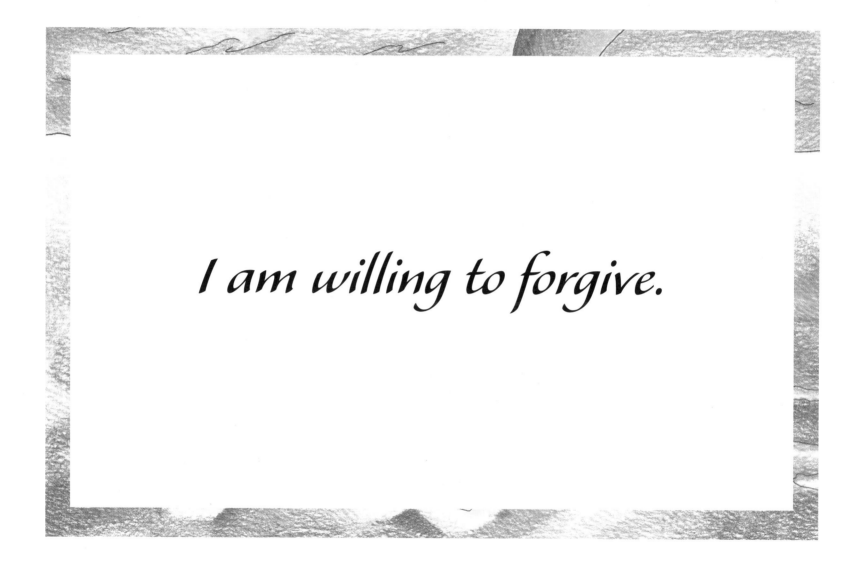

I am willing to forgive.

I am reborn.

I shine forth the peace of God.

I feel God's goodness surrounding me, making my way safe.

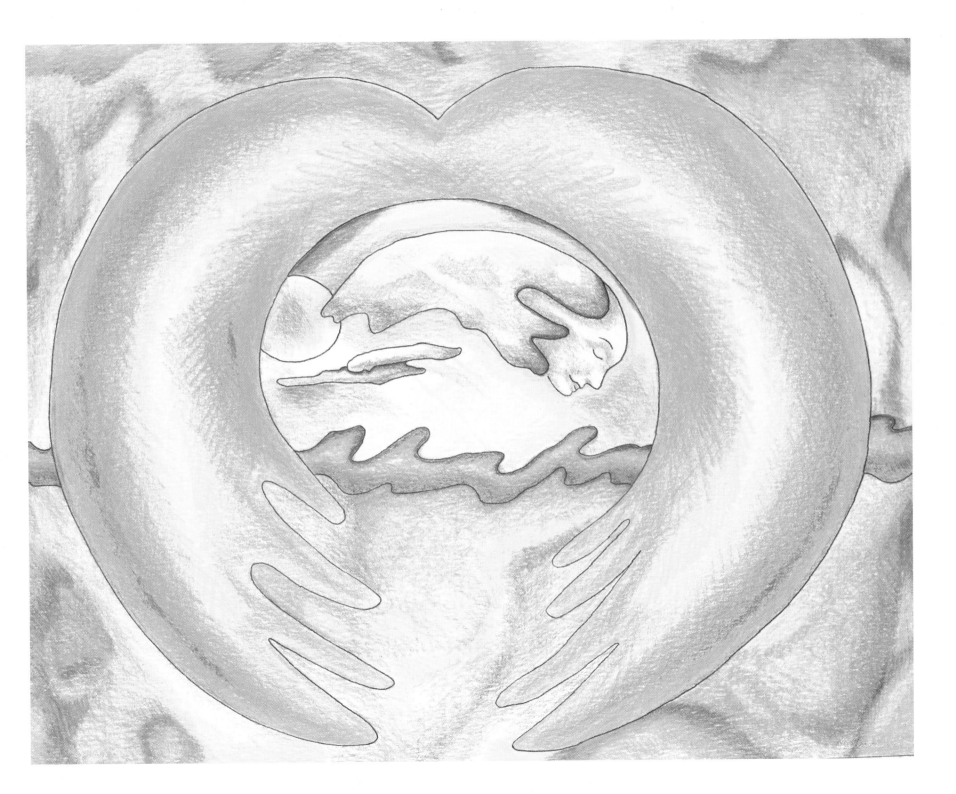

The River of Life flows gently through me.

As I rest,
my soul breathes in the Infinite.

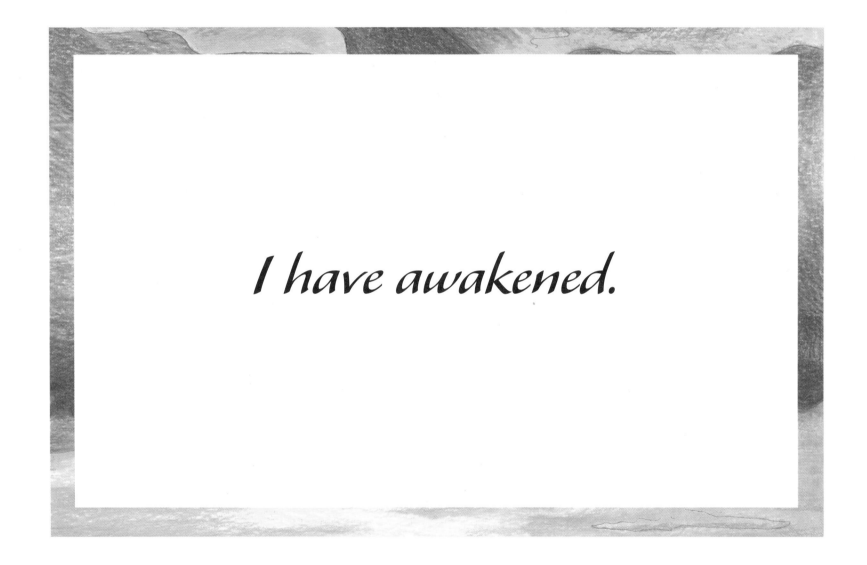

I have awakened.

*I turn to the Light
to remember who I am.*

I am a clear channel for the
Fountain of Light.

*I am living a life of beauty,
purpose, and promise.*

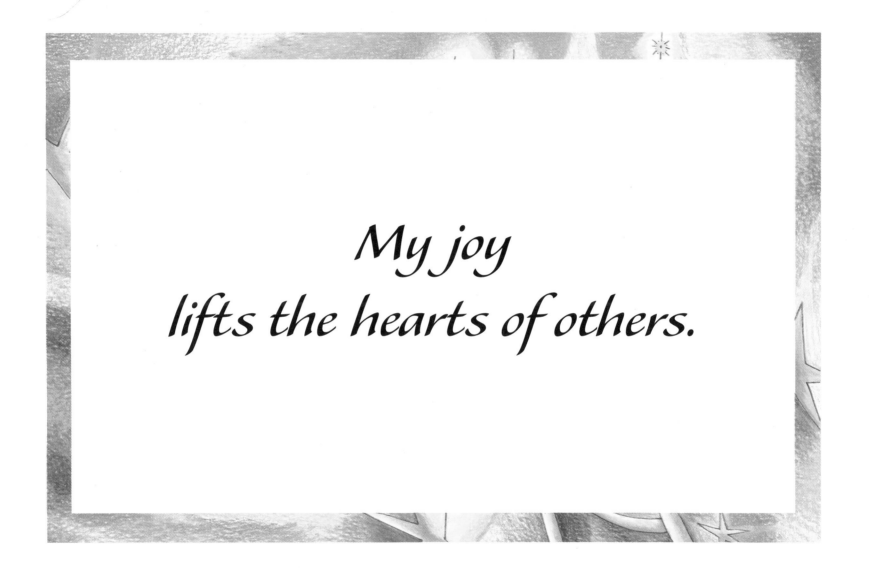

My joy
lifts the hearts of others.

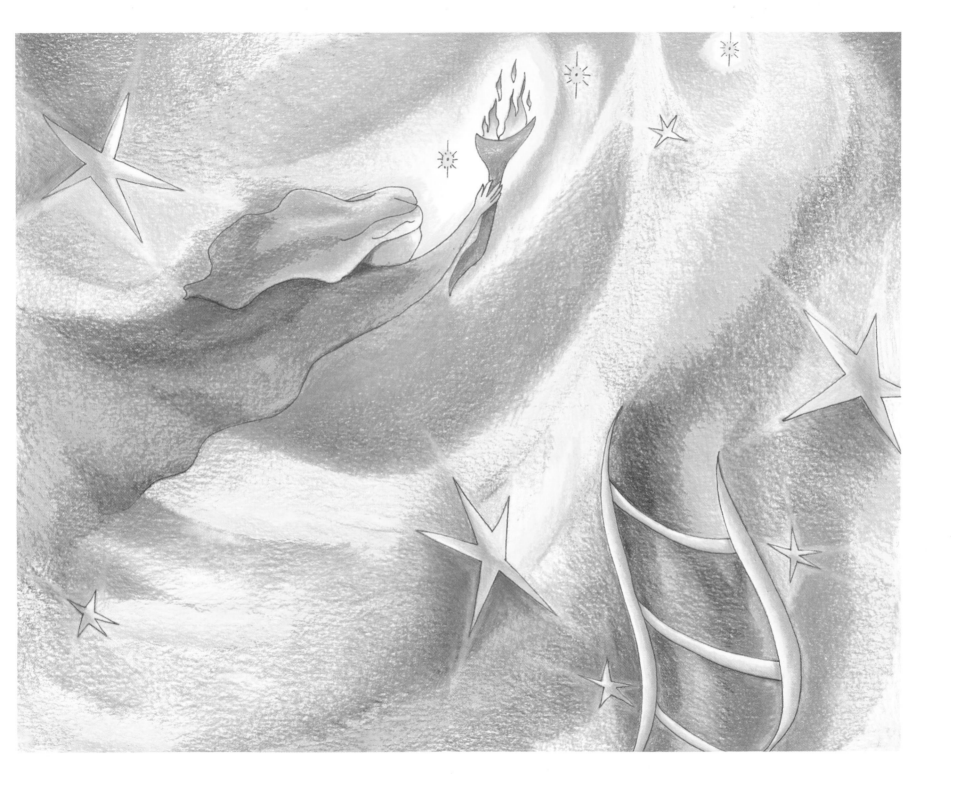

Author's Note

In the completion of this book,
I asked God, "God, how can I love You?"
And God answered: "Be true to yourself. Be true to your heart."

I asked God, "God, how can I know You?"
And God answered: "Embody that which I am; embody peace, embody gentleness,
embody Truth, embody humor and joy, and embody Love and caring and compassion."

I told God, "Thank You," and fell to my knees.
God said, "Stand up, child, for you and I are one."

About the Author

Connie Bowen began drawing at an early age and majored in art at Washington State University from 1970 to 1973. She then completed training and worked for 23 years as a free-lance court reporter.

Her first book of illustrated affirmations, *I Believe in Me*, published by Unity Books in 1995, won the national Athena Award for Excellence in Mentoring. The book continues to reach worldwide with a voice of inner strength and freedom.

Since retiring from court reporting in 1997, she has devoted full time to the loves of her life: her family, her art, and the expression of Truth. An avid student of metaphysics since 1985, she views the creation of *I Turn to the Light* as her personal journey of spiritual unfoldment and says the book presents the message of hope, the message of Love for all.

Printed in the U.S.A.   7-1502-20M-5-98